Table o

MW00595386

1) "Boys, I Just Heard A Terrible Rumor"............4

2) "Berryman Is Family"............13

3) "The New Normal"............18

4) "What Is A Palooza?"............25

5) "We Have To Do Something"............31

6) "The System is Rigged"............40

7) "Together as One"............47

8) "Am I Gonna Get Fired For This?"............55

9) "Santa Claus Is Coming To Town"............61

10)"Not A Big Retreat Guy"............70

11) "I Can't Do This"............77

1

12) "Why Is There Cake All Over The Walls".......84

13) "A Christmas Eve Like No Other".................93

14) "What The Hell Did I Just Watch...................98

15) "It's Something I Have To Do".....................104

16) "Saturdays Are For The...".............................110

17) "I'm Freezing My Ass Off Nick"...................117

18) "There's No Way That's Gonna Happen".....122

19) "You Only Get One Shot"...........................128

20) "It's Showtime"...134

21) "Building The Dream Baby".........................143

22) "It Takes A Village"...150

23)"Bigger Than Us"...157

24) "Oh It's A Show"...163

25) "So What Now"..173

A Special Thanks To Those That Helped Make This Dream a Reality

Editors Samantha Trolli and Talia Mekinulov

Diane and TJ Revelas

Will Lawley and Charlie Desmond

All of my CHS Brothers

Delia Cryan and Leah Nanna

Jimmy Kirkpatrick and Paul Cumbo

The Berryman Deadenders

Canisius High School and Nardin Elementary

"Boys, I Just Heard a Terrible Rumor"

I was sitting in my house after what had
been a very hectic couple of days. My parents and
I were fighting about what colleges to apply to,
and Christmas break was almost here. The night
before was the annual Berryman Christmas Party.
It was the most amazing time of the year, the
time of the year when families gather around the
dinner table to share their stories. The smell of
the crisp snow was beginning to linger through
the air. Christmas lights were finally lining the
streets, making the evenings feel a lot less dull. I
was ready to relax after a long week of school. I
attended Canisius High School, an all boys Jesuit

school where community values were almost as important as your grades. It felt like every school day was just another day I got to enjoy with my brothers. Even though I enjoyed school, it was time to relax. My plan for the night was to watch Christmas movies with my family and indulge in the festive cookies and chocolate milk.

As I made my way to the kitchen to make my holiday snack, I was feeling tired and a little off. I made the decision to go to bed early and get a good night's rest. As I poured my chocolate milk, my phone began to ring. I looked down and it was my best friend, Will Lawley. It wouldn't be a Saturday night without a call from my brother. I knew Will and some of my buddies were heading down to Ellicottville for the night. I assumed he

5

was just calling for a favor. I declined the call, and shortly after, my phone buzzed and Will had texted me: "you need to call me right now." Normally I would have continued to pour my chocolate milk, head to bed, and then call Will in the morning. Although on this snowy Saturday, after calling for a second time, I sensed something was wrong and called him right away.

Holding my phone close to my ear, I heard the words that will be ingrained in my mind forever, "Devin Waring killed himself tonight." In this moment everything stopped. It was as if the earth stood still. My body immediately tensed up and froze. Devin was no longer here, he wasn't here to keep me going, or do anything for that matter. The simple action of holding a cup wasn't possible anymore. The tall glass of chocolate milk slipped out of my hands and fell onto the oriental carpet. I could hear the television in the other room and my parents shouting in the distance, but the only thing on my mind was what Will was saying: "Get to Devin's right now." I stood in front of my stained carpet feeling as if a dark cloud had just washed over my whole body. I was speechless and empty. I began to walk to my room. Walking felt different than it ever had: every foot forward felt like a thousand steps backwards. My mom saw me and asked what just happened. She saw a newly formed emptiness in my eyes. I responded, "mom, my brothers are hurting, my friends need me, I have to go now."

On that dark, cold December night, thoughts began to race through my mind. It was as if nothing was real anymore, or at least I was trying to pretend it wasn't. My thoughts continued to race. Did this actually happen? Is this real right now? I kept praying that the world was playing a sick joke on me and that none of this was reality. As I was driving, all of the brothers in our group chat were saying, "Boys I just heard a terrible rumor, is it true?" One by one the texts started to pour in. Everyone was wondering what the hell was going on. It was like dominos: everything was falling down piece by piece. My body was trembling. As seconds passed by I began to come to terms with the fact that all of this madness was real. As I pulled into Devin's street, lights were flashing everywhere, but these lights did not fix the dullness that remained to linger through the night. These lights brought about chaos, and a sense of fear. This fear consumed me as I drove my car right into a neighbors mailbox, not even putting the car in park. I ran toward the house looking for any of my brothers, mostly for my brother Devin. Finally, I found one of my classmates in the sea of emergency officials. He screamed, "head over to Calog's house right now."

As the snow was falling, the walk up Calogeno's driveway felt like the longest walk of my life. It felt like weights were strapped against my ankles as it was continuing to settle in that this was real. There were cars lined up on both sides of the driveway and covering every patch of grass in sight. As I walked into the house, I saw parents and priests huddled together at the kitchen table. Downstairs was were my brothers were, all but one. The day before this we were all together in school. It was a Friday, and we were all excited for the upcoming Christmas break. Now we were here.

I was one of the first to show up but one by one everyone started to cram into Calogeno's small basement. It was a numbing feeling to watch my brothers come down to the basement. No words were needed. As people flooded the basement, everyone started hugging. The pain in the room was like nothing I've ever seen. There was an eerie silence as people were trying to process all that had happened. Once everyone arrived, people started to get up and speak to the group. Nothing was planned and nothing was written down. We were just letting out raw emotions. It took insane courage from people like our English teacher Mr Cumbo, Calogeno, and Devin's local priest to try to corral everyone's feelings and calm us down. The more they spoke, the closer we all felt, as we would be forever linked in that moment. The night waned on and I was ready to leave. I remember turning around and seeing my brothers. The people I loved making happy and the people I loved spending every day with all became lost. Everyone had developed a beam of melancholy in their eyes. I got in my car and I absolutely lost it. Seeing my brothers like that changed my life. I knew what was ahead was not going to be easy, but I would

do everything in my power to try and make things

right.

"Berryman is Family"

Some people grow up saying, "I live in the best neighborhood." I can say confidently that this is not true for others. For me, calling the dead end of Berryman Drive the best neighborhood would be an understatement. It's the kind of neighborhood where seeing grown men walk around in bikinis is a normal Saturday. It's the kind of neighborhood that will drop everything to help a fellow family in need. It's the kind of neighborhood that comes together to support their own, even if it means putting a mechanical bull on their lawn. It is more than a neighborhood. You could call it a community, but that is still wouldn't do it justice. Berryman Drive is family to me and the roots for the Fiesta Bowl started right on that block.

Growing up, my birthdays were always exciting. Christmas was just as great. Although, my absolute favorite day of the year was the Berryman Drive Block Party. It was one of those events that was so exciting that it was nearly impossible to sleep the night before. Every neighbor got involved, whether it was grilling on the road, running scavengers hunts, or turning their front lawn into a stage. The bounce houses, the bike parade, the talent show, the glow sticks hanging from the trees were all things that made the block party bigger than life.

Being part of the action was not good enough for me. I loved the idea that just from a little bit of planning, something so big and memorable could be created. This being so, in seventh grade I came up with Berryman Game Night. This was a trivia game that forced all my neighbors to squeeze into my small hot garage. It was crazy, there was usually cheating, and a whole lot of drunks yelling, but the chaos is what made me happy. The fact that everyone was smiling and engaged with one another made me proud of my creation of the game night.

Eventually, years went by and the Block Party lost some of its charm as the kids started to get older. I had to do something, seeing that it was the one and only day of the year that the entire neighborhood gathered as one. I wished for our family to come together again. I began to start coming up with ideas to try to get everyone out of their houses. I even tried raking everyone's leaves onto one lawn with the infamous Leaf Festival, which ended in several hours of clean up, and pissed off dads with leaf blowers. I tried converting our next door neighbors front lawn into a stadium. Ross, who might I add was in his mid-seventies, would come outside to spotlights on his trees and Christmas lights lining the lawn. We had street hockey seasons which converted my driveway into an arena, complete with spotlights, boards, and a trophy made of ice. After all of these efforts to bring my small street together, nothing seemed to work. It frustrated me that no matter what I did, I couldn't get the whole neighborhood together. It would take a revolutionary idea to dethrone the "event of the year."

"The New Normal"

The day after losing my brother was a brisk cold morning. I woke up and my head was as cloudy as the Buffalo sky. I did not understand what I was feeling yet. It felt like a heavy cloak had just covered my whole body. This cloak made me feel nothing, but that feeling of nothing was worse than feeling something. It was almost as if I was numb. I knew I had to clear my mind, so I decided to go for a walk. Soon enough, I noticed the weights on my ankle were still there. Once again, every step forward felt like I was pulling myself backwards. I continued to walk with weights on my ankles and a heavy cloak that dragged on the sidewalk. My body was numb.

The beams of melancholy that burst through my brothers eyes were still daggering into my heart. Feeling all of this, I continued to walk. It still had not fully processed with me that we had lost Devin. I felt as if I was already falling.

I told my parents how I was feeling and they suggested I go to the Bills game with my friend Charlie. Behind my love for Berryman Drive, my love for the Buffalo Bills was right up there. I thought it was a genius idea. Charlie Desmond, otherwise known as Dezzy, and I, got our stuff and left. It was one of the most awkward car rides of my entire life. The music was playing in the background, but that damn cloak felt like it was louder than the music. Dezzy and I tried talking but all of it was really just a blur. My mind was not focused on our conversation, but on the nothingness I still felt. By halftime the Bills were killing the Dolphins. In normal circumstances that would have me smiling ear to ear, the Bills were still in the playoff hunt and this was their year. But as much as I wanted to be happy and with my friends, I could not pretend anymore. I turned to Dezzy and said, "This just doesn't feel right, can we just go home?" This was the new normal.

Monday finally rolled around and I couldn't believe we had to go back to school. Calogeno and all the brothers agreed that going to Canisius High School that day was the right thing to do. The only thing that made me get out of bed that day was Calogeno saying, "Boys, the only way to face this is together." All of us agreed to go. We decided to get to school early for the morning mass they held daily in the chapel. I showed up to school early wanting to make sure I would be able to console all my brothers. What I did not expect when I got in the chapel, a place where before this moment I had never seen more than a dozen people in, had over two hundred students and faculty inside. I knew my friend group was hurting, but to have all of those people in their made me realize the school was just as shocked as we were. After the extremely emotional prayer service, all of us walked out to something I wouldn't have expected in my wildest dreams. Our school has always preached the idea of brotherhood, and that we are "men and women for and with others." I personally always thought that it was a corny marketing scheme, however when I came out of the chapel and saw every single teacher of our school lining the hallways, I broke into tears. I couldn't help but crying in front of my friends and my teachers. To me it felt like they were saying, "We're here for you guys," just by standing there. It was a moment of unity I will never forget.

I remember that chilling feeling walking around the hallways that day. Seeing the lost look on all the faces in the hallways. Teachers and students alike just trying to reconcile with what happened. What really surprised me was how the loss didn't just impact our friend group, but the entire school. As I sat in classes all day I was in a complete daze. Our teachers put a foot on the breaks right in the middle of studying for midterms, and let us sit and reflect. The loudest places in the school like the cafeteria, the library, and the senior lounge, were just dead silent.

I really was conflicted about going to school that day, but it ended up being a day full of healing and reflecting. I was scared to show my cloak to my brothers, but at the end of the day I knew I wasn't alone. It was like this same cloak that was placed on me was placed on top of the entire school. I got into my car and tears began streaming down my face again. My neighbor Owen got into the car, and I told him, "Days like today are why we go to this school." I knew it was going to be a long week, and I knew I had to do something to help. I needed to create something that would be able to remove this heavy, ugly

cloak that began to consume my brothers, and

replace it with something more uplifting.

"What is a Palooza?"

Before I began my journey with Canisius High School, I attended Nardin Academy. Now the reason I am going back to my elementary years is because that is when "it" all began. The idea of doing things differently than everyone else began to take shape in my time at Nardin Academy. I always liked to shake things up in and out of the classroom. I did things like bringing a dozen empanadas in for Spanish, singing "It's Raining Men," by the Weather Girls, in front of the whole school, and silly stringing one of my favorite teachers at Twitchell Palooza. I was always trying to do things that were over the top. During my last year at Nardin, I realized the only way to get things done my way was to be Nardin Class President. I saw an opportunity to show what I could do, and I took it.

The presidential election was no small feat. In the past, when I had tried to run for student council I had lost every time, always losing to more popular kids. The idea of "The System" became real to me while at Nardin, but I'll get to that later. I was running against Sam Capizzi, who was as favored as Clinton was in 2016. Sam was stoic, calm, and gave a very professional speech when he pleaded his case to the school. Then I came on. Confetti was tossed, Let's Get Loud By Jennifer Lopez blasted on all the speakers, and the crowd loved it. Going into it, everyone expected a Sam victory, but by doing things differently, I was elected president. It set the foundation that would impact the rest of my life.

One of the perks of being class president was being able to plan the annual talent show for the school. In the years prior to me, the Talent Show was starting to die. Year after year, less and less participants were involved and the future of it was at stake. My good friend Paul Koessler, my unofficial Vice President, and I were assigned with trying to revitalize the show and make it like no other.

We had to show Nardin Academy what we could do. One day Paul and I were sitting around trying to kick up ideas, and the idea came to me, let's just make it a palooza. My idea was to have the entire faculty do an act. Confetti would launch at the end (of course), and gift cards would be tossed out to the crowd, because let's be honest, who doesn't love gift cards? Paul's first response to this was "What is a palooza?" Naturally, I responded, "you'll see, big things are coming...big things Paul." Eventually, after several failed attempts, we were able to convince Mrs. Abels that confetti was a go. We were having a palooza.

The Talent Palooza was a massive success. Gift cards went flying and confetti covered the gymnasium floor. My experience of emceeing the talent show showed me a side of myself I didn't know I had. I wanted to do more. Being in front of all of those people was thrilling. That feeling of having them all at my fingertips made me realize what I loved to do. The Palooza contained a wonderful cast, made up of faculty and students. People who I still admire and love to this day. Without them I would have never been able to pull off such a successful school event. Beating the system at Nardin gave me the mental tools that helped me build the character needed to create the Fiesta Bowl.

"We Have To Do Something"

The first day back at school after the loss of Devin, my brother, was one of the most chilling experiences in my time at Canisius. When I got back to my house that night, I felt lost. I was feeling something I had never felt before. I felt like a toddler; I didn't understand how I felt and had no idea how to process it. All I knew was that I could not go through another day like that. I got home and immediately went to my bedroom. I threw my back pack in frustration and laid on my bed. It felt as if I was sinking. That same damn cloak, and those same damn weights, were still pulling me down. I felt myself turning into someone I didn't recognize. While laying down, my thoughts still raced; I had lost someone who made me who I am, how could I ever be the same? I noticed that my mind began to spiral down, thinking things that no one should think. Yet again, I felt nothing and everything at the same time. Feeling so alone, I pulled myself out of bed. Walking downstairs, one foot dragging in front of the other. I needed to talk to my parents, I knew they would be able to help.

Sitting at the dinner table, I stared at my food. I couldn't stomach the thought of eating yet. After everyone ate, everyone but me, I began to tell them all the story of my day. I told them how terrible it was, how while walking down the hallway filled with students, I still felt alone. I told them how everyone seemed to feel alone. We were all missing our brother. I explained how I didn't understand this feeling of loneliness, how could one feel so alone while being surrounded by their second family? In this moment I understood that it had to be my job to fix this any way I could. I needed to try and bring the entire senior class together, implying to my parents that we as a family had to do something to help these kids out. We had to do something to help the brotherhood stay strong. To me, this was something I had to do, not something I wanted to do. Eventually, my family and I came up with the idea to bring pizza in for all of the seniors. Later that night, thoughts raced through my head. I really hoped that something as simple as pizza could bring an entire community together. This felt like my only chance to show my brothers that we can get through this together.

Before all of the madness, the senior lounge was a place to burn off some steam. Students could walk in at anytime of the day and have a good time in the midst of stressful classes. After all of the madness, its purpose changed. Losing a brother had turned the senior lounge into a place for everyone to gather; it was a place where we felt comfortable to mourne. It's strange to think that within a moment, so much can change. The lounge used to be a place of hustling and bustling with noise and chaos. We had just gotten it opened back up after a recent cake shove, and had decorated the entire room with Christmas lights. We decided to cover the bulletin board with pictures of Devin, making it a place of unity. This allowed us to see everybody together, united as one brotherhood.

After a frantic morning, in which I texted dozens of students convincing them to spread the word, there was lunch in the senior lounge. The entire morning I was running through the motions, practicing what to say. I had to make sure I got this right; this was not a time for mistakes, I was nervous that it was all for nothing. I finally got the text saying that the pizzas had arrived. It was like nothing I had ever seen before. Twelve sheet pizzas were stacked on the front desk. Multiple people going down the hall were giving me looks. Usually this would bother me, but not on this day. A couple of students and I were bringing the pizzas down as we walked by Father Ciancimino, the President of Canisius. It was a surreal moment. In the past, he had seen me coming down that hall with cakes, ribs, dozens of breadsticks, and gift cards. He always had a look of confusion on his face. I was already a mess as is, and instead of stopping me and asking why, he nodded his head and we carried on. There was nothing to be confused about.

I was nervous the whole time getting down to the cafeteria that no one would show up, but when I walked into the room I was stunned. The senior lounge was filled to the brim. Every single senior was in the room standing and clapping as we came in. All the teachers outside in the cafeteria were confused, as the mass of the students created a booming noise. I got to the table and spoke in front of my brothers, all but one. I thanked them for coming together as one; with tears streaming down my face, I reminded them all why we were there, "Brothers Now, Brothers Forever."

I was sitting in the corner of the lounge, surrounded by all my smiling and laughing peers and I could not help but begin to think. The past couple days we had never been closer as a community. I had random students and teachers coming up to me asking if I was okay, saying they were there if I needed anything. However, I knew it was not time for me to try to snap back to normal, so naturally I just responded "okay." Out of the blue, Mr. Cumbo came up to me. He saw the lost look on my face, and the bags under my eyes and asked me, "Nick are you sure you're okay?" It was the first time I really self evaluated, the first time that I took a step back and stopped focusing on others. I realized I had not slept or eaten in days, but none of that really mattered to me. My parents gave me the chance to change the narrative for a few minutes. Their small act of kindness gave me hope that we would all get through this together, as one. It wasn't about thank you's or getting recognized, it was that for those couple of minutes, everyone could forget and smile.

"The System is Rigged"

At this point, the real question is what is the system? It isn't a single person, a group, or even Canisius as a whole. It is every person who has told me that I'm "not good enough," that I "can't do it," and "that will never happen." During my four years, I faced more adversity than some people face in a lifetime. Canisius enabled me to face a four year character building battle against the system, and win it.

At the start, I knew high school would not be easy. The transition into freshman year was not going to be a smooth ride. On top of finding friends and getting used to a new school, my grades at Nardin were never great. This made the transition not only socially pressuring, but academically as well. Freshman year ended up being significantly worse than I could have ever imagined. Soon enough I was required to go to the counselor's office weekly about bad grades. This created a bad running joke amongst my classmates every morning that I got the yellow counselor pass. I had to stay after and meet with teachers daily, and my parents were forced to hire a tutor. It was a mess as soon as I heard the words: "Welcome class of 2018." After my freshman year I ended up going to summer school for Algebra.

I went into sophomore year with parents who only had the highest of expectations. I was already meeting with a tutor throughout the summer, and it was starting to ruin my afternoon pool sessions. After what felt like the longest six weeks of my life, summer school was finally done and I knew it was something I never wanted to go through again. I learned the hard way that in math skills build off from preexisting skills, and since I didn't know Algebra well, Geometry was going to be yet another bumpy road. By the time I got to midterms, my grades were near record lows. There was a point were I got placed on academic probation, which barred me from being on the swim team, only making me feel less and less motivated to keep trying. My parents and I started to get in more and more arguments, resulting in a family meeting with the assistant principal. My parents discussed leaving Canisius to go to Amherst High School if things didn't change soon. Scared by the idea of leaving all my brothers, I attempted a ferocious second half comeback, but I had already dug myself in too big of a hole, and ended up failing a second time by only one point.

Going into junior year, expectations were extremely high. A bar was set, seeming so high that I could never reach it. My parents and I both knew that colleges were going to be seeing my transcripts, and that I needed a big year to help my damaged stats. Yet again, it all started to become a running joke that I attended back to back years of summer school. It was a tough time knowing how much work needed to be done to try to fix things. These jokes only made me shrink, making it seem physically impossible to reach the high bar set by my parents. Trigonometry seemed like a foreign language, and it finally felt like I had found my match. I found it hard to even pass tests and quizzes. Not only was math a sinking ship, but chemistry turned out to be the Titanic. My entire year was a battle against trying to survive those two courses. I failed Trigonometry and Chemistry; and it wasn't even close. I was now going to summer school for two courses, and I was officially now back for the third consecutive year. The jokes started going around again: "Go Kat's," referring to the mascot of the community college in Buffalo. After failing to keep my promise that this year would be the year, times became tough. I had already gone through being the laughing stock and I knew how to handle it. Although this defeat was personal to me. I felt like I let my whole family down. I felt that they blew three years of tuition money on me. To make things even worse, the timing of summer school was right in the middle of my planned family trip. I was forced to stay home and miss spending time with my family. I looked at summer school as another test from the system. Being able to overcome adversity like this has helped me build the character I needed to accomplish everything I do.

"Together As One"

As the week crept on, I became more grateful of my surroundings. It is strange how a tragedy can bring people together. I had never had to rely on people as much as I did in these times. I realized how thankful I was for my parents. They did not force anything on me, they just tried to be there for me. I appreciated my sisters more than I ever had. Even though they were struggling with the situation as well, they still came in my room to check on me. I appreciated my neighbors who brought over cookies and came to check in. They sent texts and letters saying they were there for us in that rough time. However, most of all, I appreciated my brothers. Don't get me wrong, we were close as a group before all of this happened, but soon enough our group chat became the only the thing I cared to look at. Every text I opened was proof for how much we all loved each other, making each day a little easier to get through.

I also realized how grateful I was for choosing to go to Canisius High School. At our freshman orientation we all saw that our slogan was Brothers Now, Brothers Forever. I did not know what the hell that meant. Honestly, I looked at the whole brotherhood thing as a big ploy, and something Canisius put on brochures. It took almost the full four years for me to understand that slogan, and it made perfect sense after that week. Administrators, teachers, and other students across the whole school shut down for a whole week to help the seniors get through our emotions. It was truly an amazing thing to see.

One day I got an email from my counselor. She wanted to see me after other students had noticed I was having a hard time with this. We talked for what seemed like hours. It was just a mess of pent up stress and emotion finally coming out. It was amazing. I had yet to talk about anything I felt. I told her I planned to write a letter to the school thanking them for everything they had done, and why coming together as a school is what makes Canisius special. That was never more evident than the basketball game Tuesday night.

My Tuesday night started off down at Cornerstone City Mission serving dinner to dozens of families, something my family does every year for the holidays. It was the first time seeing my grandmother and my sister, who was returning from college in Boston. It was great seeing everybody, but even my mom knew my mind wasn't clear at that point. I was going through the motions, barely able to keep my head up, or talk to the patrons. I couldn't focus on anything but my brothers. My mom saw this, and let me leave early to head to the big basketball game, to be with my brothers.

Canisius vs Irondequoit was one of the most highly anticipated matchups of the year. The game was at Canisius, and word was spreading for everyone to come to the game. I walked into the field house and there was over two hundred of our students. It was one of the largest crowds I had ever seen for a basketball game in my four years at Canisius. Devin's younger brother, Owen, surprised all of us with his bravery and courage that day. Owen was front and center of our infamous Blue Crew student section. A patriotic theme was in place to honor Devin, and after the moment of silence we all sang the national anthem, together as one brotherhood. I knew there was no way in hell we were losing that game.

A back and forth battle ensued for the next hour as we were trailing in points most of the game. In the fourth quarter, with only a few minutes left, we were able to tie it up. The anticipation was building and the atmosphere was amazing. Every one of my brothers was finally focused on something else. This was all

I wanted to see, even if it would only last as long as the game did. Those final few minutes we screamed as loud as we could; the energy was contagious. We were being so loud that it was nearly impossible for others around us to hear each other. In the final minute, we took the lead and were able to hang on and win the game. We all stormed onto the court. It didn't just feel like the basketball team won, but that the entire school had won. For the victory chant, Owen Waring was lifted on people's shoulders and led the entire Blue Crew. It was one of the most chilling, surreal moments of my entire life. After the game was over, I remember getting in my car and breaking down into tears. Something as trivial as a basketball game not only brought us together, but healed us all for a little bit. For a couple of hours we forgot all that had happened, we got to be seniors in high school again. It truly was my favorite moment in my entire time at the school.

"Am I Gonna Get Fired For This?"

It can't be argued that high school is a stressful time for a majority of students. As a student, we are expected to get good grades, make sure we get into college, and be a happy kid at the same time. I am not saying that college was not important to me, but I hate the concept of being defined by a set of numbers. I went into school every day trying to break the norm. I tried my hardest to create those moments that would make kids go home and say, "Mom you won't believe what I saw today!" Therefore, as the academic struggles continued, my drive to make school days more fun and exciting soared. My focus was not on numbers, but on the memories that I was constantly making with my brothers.

My entire drive to try to shake things up at Canisius started in Mr Hinchcliffe's class. "Hinch" was my favorite teacher during my freshman and sophomore year. His class was the perfect environment to try and do things a little differently. I went into his office and proposed Hinchweek: an entire week where school work went out the window. School work would be replaced with games and gift cards being tossed. The first words out of his mouth were, "Am I going to get fired for this?" Obviously, no teacher in their right mind would agree to this. After hours of conniving, Hinch and I decided I would pass out food at the beginning of class, but that was the extent of the fun. Although I wasn't satisfied with his response. I knew that no one would get excited about this, and that I could do more. I made a powerpoint for the idea, and after getting it approved, I added slides that included things like homework passes, and Dinosaur BBQ being brought in. By the time Hinch realized what was going on, gift cards were being tossed and it was a total scene. I went down to the front doors to pick up the Dino, and the receptionist had a lost look in her eyes. Container after container of ribs and pulled pork were piled on the desk. Mr. Hinchcliffe taught me to pursue everything you believe in, no matter what it takes, a skill which became vital in my future endeavors.

My great relationship with Mr. Hinchcliffe continued for other events, like Hinchmas. This was a day filled with waffles being cooked in the room and syrup covering the floors. We even convinced Hinch to arm wrestle a student, an event which shut down the entire second floor of the building, eventually getting the dean of students involved.

Things like that did not only occur in Mr Hinchcliffe's class, and my reputation started to grow. Canisius had never seen anything like it. Latin class morphed into Latin De Mayo, complete with over a hundred breadsticks from Olive Garden. Presentations about the decline of the wild buffalo population in Biology included tickets to the local baseball games. Mr Siuta's history class became SiutaFest, and included things like chia pets and gift cards under people's desks. Homeroom would include weekly trips to bring hot chocolate and donuts to kids. Secret Santas and cakes with our teachers faces on them became the norm at Canisius. There was even a morning when we set up six toasters and cooked waffles for the entire third floor of the building. It got to the point that when classes started junior year, kids got excited when they found out I was in their class. They knew that that would mean prizes were on there way.

I always wanted to be "that guy," the person people could count on if they were having a tough day, and the person that would get things done if needed. It began to feel like hosting these events would make people say, "oh that's the kid that tosses gift cards." Putting a smile on people's faces became my number one desire. The mantra, that was known as "The Show," is what I wanted to be every time I walked into 1180 Delaware. The more I started planning these events for others, the less I was caring about myself and things I wanted. This was something that affected me later on and continues to still.

"Santa Claus Is Coming To Town"

Imagine the pressure of trying to lift an entire school's morale after what had been the worst week of school ever... that's what I had on my shoulders. As the school week neared the end, everyone was looking toward the half day Thursday. Tom Blumberg, Sam Capizzi, and a couple of other students from Student Senate were presented to make the annual Christmas video for the student body. At the beginning of December, I looked at it as an honor when they asked me to be a part of the team. Up to that point, we had made an incredible video. It included the entire senior class causing complete chaos by creating a small riot in the library. Although, after the loss of Devin everything came to a screeching halt. Tom, Sam and I were extremely close to Devin, so when other students suggested we got back to filming, it was something we couldn't do whole-heartedly. It became very tough to get through the scenes. We handed in the video at the last possible minute, and were not really sure what was going to happen next.

When all of us met to discuss our plan for the presentation Thursday, we knew it was going to be an extremely difficult day. We had school for half of the day, but later that afternoon we were all going to Devin's wake, something that I still could not fathom was going to happen. We came up with the idea that I was going to dress up as Santa, and try to hype up all the students. I was even going to get a chance to tackle Mr. Coppola. All of this meant I was responsible for openly trying to spread joy in the midst of sorrow and loss. This became very difficult; it almost made me feel uncomfortable. Why would I be forcing joy onto hundreds of mourning kids? We knew it was going to be hard to convince people that coming to school that morning was the right thing to do, but I remember telling the other kids in the room that: "We have an opportunity to change the narrative for all of these kids, even if it's for an hour we got to give it everything we got." Every kid got on their phone and texted everybody they knew to show up to school the next day. Heading home, I remember telling my dad: "We got some shopping to do." My dad was fully supportive of me, and he knew that this meant a lot to all the kids at school. Supporting me meant going to six different stores to find a Santa costume, gift cards, and of course the staple of every Nick Revelas presentation: Juicy Fruit.

The School's mission seemed to be trying get kids in the Christmas spirit. It was a brisk Tuesday and everyone was dressed in red and green from head to toe. The buzz went up and down the hallways as kids walked from homeroom to homeroom exploring the different food spreads. Rolling my Santa filled suitcase into the senior lounge, I just tried to get away from everyone. I was still not ready to accept that things were back to normal. I placed my headphones on and looked around. Kids were laughing, smiling, and just trying to have a good time. Meanwhile, in my head I was still extremely nervous about the idea of dressing up as Santa. I sat there in a curled up ball saying to myself "Is this the right thing to do or is it too soon for this?" Suddenly, Father Ciancimino came out of the blue and said, "Nick I heard you're going to be dressing up as Santa Claus, is that true?" After replying yes, I explained I'd also be tackling Mr. Coppola to try and create excitement. After a look of confusion, he said, "You only get one shot, so it better be worth it."

As we were walking towards the auditorium, one by one students and teachers were coming up to me saying things like, "Give em hell today Rev," "You got this Nick," and "Santa Claus is coming to town." It was hard not to break down when I saw that I had that kind of support from the school, more importantly the brotherhood. It gave me the confidence I needed; finally I felt like I was gonna kill it. We started the assembly by having all of the seniors walk in with lit candles into the dark auditorium. This symbolized the situation perfectly. Even though we were all in the dark, we still had the power to bring light. Walking to my seat, I realized that today was an opportunity to bring light into a dark situation. Finally, I knew that this was the right thing to do.

The second Mr. Coppola introduced the Christmas video, I went running out of my seat. I knew I only had a few minutes to change from my button down and khakis into a full Santa costume up in the library. Luckily, I was able to get changed and run downstairs right before my cue. When Mr. Coppola walked to the stage to introduce me, I came running down the aisle. A lot was going through my head. I saw the look of the confused freshman and sophomores and could see the senior class in the front going berserk. I let out all that pent up anger, stress, and emotion that had been with me those past few days when I tackled Mr. Coppola. It was absolute pandemonium, and when I got up off the ground, a standing ovation was initiated.

A few hours before, I was so afraid to do this, and it ended up being the thing I'm most proud of doing to this day. I ran around, tossed some gift cards, and chirped some of my teachers that sent me to summer school. It might have only been for an hour, and what was to come next was going to be tough, but at that moment we became one Canisius. This was something no one could ever take away from us.

"Not A Big Retreat Guy"

Part of what makes my high school

unique from any other in the area is the

campus ministry. They offer the best trips to

students to go around the world and help those

in need. They also have retreats for the

students that are focused on self improvement.

I was pretty cynical about going and did not

really understand the benefit of it, but my

parents forced me to. At the end of junior year,

I decided to embark on a three day retreat at

Lake Erie, known as Kairos. After finding out I

was going with several close friends, like

Spencer and Troy, I was pretty excited to be

missing school for a couple of days. It was a critical point for me in my life. Academically, I felt I had blown three years of premium high school education, a lot of my parent's time, and money. Socially, I knew I was surrounded by a good group of guys, but I did not really feel that close to any of them. The mantra of "Revelas against the System" was in full effect. I really felt like there was so much was in the way for me to succeed, which made it hard to trust anybody, even those who I was closest to.

Two days had passed, and frankly I was confused about the whole thing. I know I'm not a big retreat guy, but it seemed like the entire thing is sitting around in a circle and talking about feelings. There was even a point in which the retreat leaders asked everyone to write down their sins on a card and throw them in the fire. I was the only one not to do it. I felt like a square peg trying to fit in a round hole, and I genuinely thought that this was the biggest waste of time. Although, it was when I arrived home that I realized that there was a purpose to this trip. I was greeted at home by a letter wrapped in an envelope laying on my desk. This letter, written by my parents, eventually shifted my entire perspective of life.

My parents and I had not always gotten along as smooth as other families. There was a lot of yelling and shouting matches. This gave my dad the infamous reputation amongst all of my friends as "T Heavy." Especially over the last few months prior to Kairos, things had hit the boiling point with another year of summer school being inevitable. Fights were breaking out every day with my family members. It was really at that point where I felt like I was letting my family down, and that I had wasted away all of the gifts that they bestowed upon me. They were there for me financially for Fiesta Bowls, buying breadsticks and gift cards for school, and pretty much anything I'd ask for, but the one thing they wanted was for me to become a successful student. People began to think college was not even going to be an option for me, but when I opened the letter from them, they didn't talk about the fights, the bad grades, or all the disappointments. The letter ended very clearly: "We're rooting for you Nick, you got this." It absolutely shook to me to my core. Despite all the crap we'd been through as a family they were still my biggest fans.

The letter did more than just let me know my parents still had the faith in me to turn things around; it changed my entire stance on "The System." I had grown into a person that was more jaded and cynical than ever before. Every person that said I couldn't do it, along with every bad grade I received, only created more internal frustration. I knew that I only had my senior year to turn things around. I wanted to turn things around academically, so I could finally prove to my parents and everyone that I will get into a great college. Socially, I wanted to try to make every day the best I could, by helping even more people. This meant more community service and doing more things at school to try to expand "The Show" brand. Personally, I knew that this was my last chance to try to make a real difference. It was my time to show my brothers, my family and everyone in my corner that I can do this. I knew if I was going to accomplish all of this senior year, I was going to have to do

something extravagant.

"I Can't Do This"

Following the rambunctious Christmas assembly, my head could not stop ringing. It was unbelievable. My head was held high after leaving school, and I was really happy about what we did, but I knew that would only last a few short hours. Heading to Devin's wake was something I could not believe. It would only make everything more real than it already was. Just six short days ago, he was in class with us. How was I on my way to see him in a casket?

We pulled into the funeral home and saw the sea of people winding down the street. It was freezing, and even started snowing at points, but we all remained quiet with our heads down. Reality still had not set in. The wait seemed like hours, but eventually I got to kneel on the stool and pay my respects. After days of trying to avoid the feeling of being hurt and accepting the facts, it finally hit me. This was real and Devin is gone. I left the small room to go outside and saw dozens of my classmates. The sense of brotherhood had never been stronger. With everyone hugging and consoling one another, it felt like we were all a family. Leaving the funeral home I tried to clear my head of things and went to dinner with some friends. While everyone was eating and laughing, I sat there frozen with the thought of Devin in a casket in my head. I got home and did not sleep a minute. I continued to think about the look on all my brother's faces, and how much it hurt me to know I really could not help them.

The funeral was held a few days later. Just as before, I made my way into the crowded church. This was a unique moment, and an experience I will never forget. As I walked up the aisle, I passed pew after pew filled with students. Almost the entire senior Canisius class was there, along with a large portion of the faculty. Not only was my brotherhood right there, but there were more and more kids coming in that did not attend

Canisius. It was surreal to think that my entire brotherhood was gathered for the purpose of one of our brother's funeral. The service was filled with tears, prayers, and reflection. My close friends Calogeno and Troy showed incredible bravery doing one of the readings. Everyone in the room felt the power of the moment. I broke down as his casket left the church. It felt like he was leaving all of us. As they carried the casket out of the door, they carried a part of each and everyone of us with them. That cold and rainy morning cars lined up and began heading to the burial. The cars stretched for what seemed like miles. Police officers and cars directed traffic all the way to the cemetery. As we gathered, it all ended with each of us placing a rose on the casket, and just like that, it was over. How could it be? I knew it was not over for me, or anyone else in that room. It was the beginning of a new way. A goal of mine had always been making sure everyone was happy from time to time, but after this moment, my new goal changed into making sure everyone was happy during the future moments that they experienced.

My parents wanted us to have a family dinner. They invited our close family friends, the Desmonds, to try to clear our heads after what had been a long week. I remember anxiously waiting for the dinner to finish, so I could head out to Calogeno's. When I walked into Calogeno's basement, the scene was unexpected. Kids were playing beer pong, pouring drinks, laughing, smiling and having a good time. Externally it looked like everyone in the room was recovering and seemed to be having fun. Internally, I just could not accept the situation for what it was. I could not sit down and enjoy myself with the people I love. It felt like I hadn't done enough for everyone and there was still something that I could do. After I brought some party favors for the kids, I stayed for fifteen minutes and really did not feel like I fit in, so I got up to walk out. Some of my closest friends: Calogeno, Delia, Leah and Will, were all wondering where I was going, and I told them "I'm sorry, I can't do this." Healing is different for everybody, and when I got into my car I felt obligated to try to think of something to help these people that were family to me.

"Why Is There Cake All Over The Walls"

Heading into senior year, I had set extremely high expectations for myself. It had been a challenging junior year, and after going to summer school twice, I knew I was not taking a math or science. I knew that my relationships with teachers throughout the school were reaching their peak, and that since I was a detention free student, I'd be able to get the favors needed to shake things up. Most importantly I knew this was going to be the last year I got to be with my friends, some of which I had been going to school with since the third grade. The idea of everyone splitting up for college scared me a little bit, and so I knew I wanted to do everything I could to make each day special in and out of the classroom.

The blue crew was the fan section of our high school, and was something I always wanted to be a leader of. Being one of the kids in the front row leading the chants seemed like the perfect job for me. But in my first three years I really did not take the opportunities in front of me, like joining the blue crew club, or going to all the games. So with some close friends officially in charge of it, I got my chance to take a bigger role in things. Pregames for football included things like sliding freshman down slip n slides and throwing hot dogs in peoples cars. But it always ended with Tom, Sam and I getting on top of a car giving a pep talk to the students. Nothing got me more fired up then when we were screaming at the top of our lungs, gift cards were being tossed, and the crowd was going absolutely insane. It felt like I was finally fitting in with students that I normally wouldn't talk to, and it help strengthen the bond I had with the students in my senior class.

Another opportunity I passed up on in my time at Canisius was joining student senate, and it was something I regretted deeply. The student senate members were the only ones that got to speak in front of the students when it came to assemblies and pep rallies. So when I heard the opportunity to join the Walkathon club I hopped right on board.

The Walkathon was the yearly event that encouraged students to raise money for the school, and it also included a massive presentation to pitch the event to the entire school. Run by the assistant dean Mr Flaherty and a group of junior and senior students, they selected me to be the MC for the pitch. At the

87

time I thought this may be the only chance I get to talk to the whole student body, so I was going to have to do it big. I went into Mr Coppola's office, the dean of the school, to pitch what I wanted to do. I told him wild ideas of intro songs, gift cards, and involving the students. One of the lessons I learned is that the journey may be tough at times, and you face a lot of road blocks, but don't ever let deter you from your goals. The presentation got approved, it went off without a hitch, and

getting that jubilation from the crowd made me so excited for what was to come.

Senior year also gave me the unique privilege of having a senior lounge, a small room in the cafeteria where everyone would gather during breaks and free periods. It was basically a place for me to bring things in without any consent needed. So it did not take long for me to realize that this would be the perfect place to keep doing the things I loved, but on an even bigger level. But that ended shortly as the lounge was closed for it being too messy. This started my very close relationship throughout the year with Mr Coppola and Mr Flaherty. I had never had detention or anything like that, so I really did not have a great relationship, but I was able to negotiate and get the lounge back open, by agreeing to get a vacuum. After telling my mom I needed "money for a school project", I went up to Walmart and brought in a new vacuum and some decorations and the lounge was open the next day. I would bring in Bills flags, cover the entire room in Christmas lights, really do whatever I could to try to spice things up from what can be a very boring school day at times.

My boldest idea to try to get people excited in the senior lounge was a cake shove. The night before I went to the grocery store for another "school project", and bought two cakes and used some of my lawn mowing money and got some gift cards. I started hyping it up that night by texting everybody in the class to meet in the senior lounge at lunch. When I walked into the lounge it was mostly a look of confusion on the kids' faces when I walked in with birthday cakes. I started screaming to everybody "Whoever shoves this cake in their face gets a $25 dollar visa." People went absolutely ballistic, everyones hands were waving wanting to be picked and people outside the lounge were starting to peek through the windows. Eventually we got two victims, they got their heads shoved in cake, and it looked like people were having some fun. That woud not last because by the time lunch was over, and I was scrubbing the floors clear of cake, Mr Coppola was standing over me. He said "Why is their cake all over the walls", and I tried explaining to him the idea of the cake shove and it made me realize outside looking in, this must sound crazy. Mr Coppola and I had formed a good relationship following the Walkathon and other senior lounge madness, which would be pivotal in the upcoming months.

"A Christmas Eve Like No Other"

After what had felt like the longest week of my life, it was finally Christmas Eve. The entire lead-up to Christmas had been completely overshadowed by everything going on. It surprised the hell out of me when my mom came into my room saying, "Nick it's time to wake up we're going to Uncle Matt's." When I went into the bathroom I took a look into the mirror and really analyzed myself. I had bags under my eyes and I felt like a zombie from not sleeping all week. My stomach looked inverted from skipping so many meals, and my voice was extremely hoarse. Mentally and physically, all of this stress had taken a toll on me. I was hoping that Christmas Eve with my extended family would help.

We got to Matt and Gail's and I felt like everyone was speaking a foreign language. They tried to be nice, and gave the classic, "Nick I'm really sorry about your friend." I knew that they all cared, but at the same time none of them could understand what was really going on. Savannah and I sat on the couch, watching everyone smiling and excited to be together, but it really did not feel right to be in the holiday spirit. One of the most celebrated traditions at a Murphy Family Christmas is right at the end when all of the Murph's get together say their favorite moment of the year. People talked about graduations, summer picnics, even a fishing trip. I had no idea what I was going to say, so when everyone turned to hear Savannah go first, I was stunned with what I heard. Savannah came out and said:

"My favorite moment of the year was one that I wasn't actually there for. The other night at Devin's house I heard everyone was really struggling with the news of our friend Devin. My friends told me Nick was able to calm everyone down and help, and that made me really proud to call Nick my brother."

There was not a dry eye in the room when Savannah spoke. My parents, aunts and uncles all looked on me with my head buried in my lap, tears pouring down my face. My sister and I had never had a close relationship. There were a lot of arguments and nicknames, and even a fight in the middle of a crowded beach. However, this past week had been the closest we had ever been. Hearing her talk like that changed our relationship forever. By the time I was up to speak only one emotion was going through my head: love. Love is something we take for granted every day, but it was the only thing that got me through that tough week. It was the love of my family that supported me through anything I needed to do. It was the love of my neighbors that were there for me when I really felt alone. Most importantly, it was the love of my brothers that's what got me through it; all of us coming together is something that made me so proud. My classmates really felt like my family from there on out. I knew from that point on, as I was driving back home, that I had to take care of these people that had taken such good care of me. I just had to think of something that could bring us all together.

"What the Hell Did I Just Watch"

I had always tried to think of something that would compliment my neighborhood Block Party, but deep down I realized that my goal was to create something bigger than what the dead end had ever seen, and dethrone the Block Party as the event of the year. One day, my neighbor, Jimmy Kirkpatrick, and I were playing basketball, a sport neither of us knew how to play, but one that brought out a bitter rivalry nonetheless. It was right there and then that we decided that we would create the Fiesta Bowl. A one on one basketball game that would pit Jimmy and I against each other in front of the whole neighborhood. Although, we both knew that basketball alone would not bring everyone together, so we came up with random activities, like three legged races, a polar bear mascot, and most importantly, the full service bar.

In the early years, the focus was not really on the game, but more on the hot tub construction workers. There were conversations filled with controversies on topics like everyone paying for bright neon shirts. The support of the neighbors was one thing, but I wanted to make it bigger than just our little dead end.

After the second year, the future of the Fiesta Bowl was a little murky. It would take a tragedy to give the Fiesta Bowl a bigger meaning than basketball. Dante Lasting was more than a neighbor, he was one of my closest friends. When I heard the news of his mom contracting early onset Alzheimer's, it shook our entire community. The term, "Berryman is Family" was never more true than in this troubling time; people showed constant support for the Lastings. We all understood what we had to do.

I felt personally obligated to try to do whatever I could do to help the Lastings. I soon realized I needed to start focusing on other families going through the same thing as well, and we decided that we would raise money for Alzheimer's. Jimmy and I also decided in the third year of the Fiesta Bowl that we needed to try and ramp up the excitement for the event by making significant changes. We changed the format to a three on three, so that people didn't just have to watch thirty minutes of complete garbage. We added my uncle, John Murphy, who is the voice of the Buffalo Bills, and we decided to open the event more to the public by inviting close family and friends.

People were absolutely stunned while coming up the street. There were banners hanging across the road, VIP parking signs drilled into the trees, and a massive American flag planted across the roof. It was when my Uncle John saw a polar bear running around the driveway, he came up to me and said "I'm really not sure what this is." Even some of my closest friends, the "Dead Enders of Berryman Drive", came out and told my parents, "What the hell did I just watch?" The event went off without a hitch; people were both confused and amazed at the same time, which was the original goal. Nothing made me happier than the moment after my speech. Being able to go find Mrs. Lasting and tell her we did it gave me a feeling of accomplishment greater than anything I had ever felt. I sat in my driveway, which was covered with confetti, and held the championship trophy in my hand. I thought to myself that the Fiesta Bowl was clearly something that would work. I knew it would only get better with the years to come.

"It's Something I Have To Do"

After a Christmas morning, I felt weak in the stomach opening Christmas presents. We were preparing for our trip to Florida, but the only thing on my mind for the past few days was how I was going to help my friends. I thought about how the Fiesta Bowl the year prior was able to bring the whole neighborhood together in just one day, and I wanted to keep that momentum going into this year. The only difference was that this time it was not just a neighborhood we were trying to help and heal, but an entire community.

I brought my parents down into my small basement and I told them that at this year's event we were going to raise as much money as possible for depression, an issue I had never even thought about before a few weeks ago. Most importantly, I explained to them that this is something I have to do and that people are going to be looking towards us to try to create something that can heal a hurt community. I pitched the goals I had come up with: raise ten thousand dollars, have over 200 people, and create a three on the three tournament, which was something we had never tried before. The year prior we were only able to raise one thousand dollars for Alzheimer's, and had only entertained about 75 people. I knew my parents were the original believers because when I spoke, they did not flinch. Although most people would have laughed or said you're out of your mind, the first thing out of my parents' mouths were ideas and solutions, not concerns. After a couple hours hashing out details, the plan was set and I really thought this was going to be something that no one had ever seen. However, as I sat in my room happy and content that my parents were on board, I could not help but flashback to the night that we lost Devin.

That night in Calogeno's basement, what started as screaming and tears, turned into a room full of quiet teenagers, who had all lost

their innocence in a span of hours. People had

given their speeches, and it was now time to

sit back and reflect. Before I walked out the

door, teary eyed and just lost, I knew I wanted

to talk to Calogeno and Troy. We gathered in

the tiny laundry room away from all the chaos

for a minute, and I made a promise for them

and everyone before I left. I told them "I will

do everything I possibly can to make things

better, no matter what it takes." I may have

been emotion-filled and delirious from

everything going on, but I knew that when I

make a promise, I don't back down on it. I

spent every day with those kids in that

basement going to school for the last four

years. They were family to me, and I knew that I had to be there for them the most in these difficult times.

I sat in my basement with a plan in front of me to really try to make a difference, to try something that had never been attempted before, and something that I never even thought was possible. All the years of making people happy with gift cards, and parties, and anything I could, was going to come down to this. My parents knew to an extent that the Fiesta Bowl meant a lot to me, but they didn't know that this meant everything to me. In the next few months a college choice would be made and graduation would occur, but all of that was going to be pushed to the side. I felt the pressure on my shoulders of trying to help everyone and make a difference. Maybe it was wrong to put all of this on myself, but it felt like something I had to do. The system had tested my will before with summer school, family fights, and everyone who had doubted me, but this would be the toughest test yet.

"Saturday's Are For The..."

My relationship over the past few years with my family had been interesting to say the least. There were not many days where my parents and I didn't argue about something, and my relationships with my sisters were heavily strained. I knew that I would be leaving for college this upcoming year, and looked at the Fiesta Bowl as an opportunity to bring us all a little closer as a family. I also knew the magnitude of this year's event would be a greater challenge than I had ever faced. The idea of the Fiesta Bowl bringing my family closer started to resonate with me over the winter break. One of the nights at dinner when I explained to my sisters how we were going to need all hands on deck, they were all on board and willing to lend a helping hand.

When we got back from break I knew the grind would start right away.. Saturdays in my house usually consisted of an hour dedicated to arguing about grades, manual labor out or around the house, and my dad watching four to six hours of Law and Order on the couch. Therefore when it came time to work on the Fiesta Bowl, Saturdays became a full fledged family affair.

We would FaceTime my sister Ari, who was in school in Boston, and she would be work on the website and all the PR pieces. My other sister was pitching to every single one of her friends, left and right, to get donations. My mom was in charge of all the financials, and also was trying to keep the Fiesta Bowl under budget for the first time in history. My dad was going company to company, trying to get money from sponsors and spread the word about the event. Even my grandmother went into stores trying to convince businesses to join the cause. Saturdays are normally "for the boys", but my senior year I was all in on June 9th.

It was during one of these meetings, that just from a simple google search, we were able to find a charity to donate to. Depression and suicide were issues I had never thought of before, and were things I had never been taught how to deal with. By literally typing on my laptop, "depression care buffalo," I was able to find Horizon Health Services. We were able to get a hold of them, and they were actually willing to sit down and hear about our big, crazy idea. I was pretty nervous going in because pitching to teachers about throwing gift cards in their room is one thing, but proposing the Fiesta Bowl in front of the CEO of Horizon was a lot more intimidating. The whole day leading up to the meeting everyone was trying to tell me what to say, and how to convince them. I had never let people dictate the way I make decisions in the past, so I ignored the noise and went with my gut.

Instead of talking about all the material things, like the mascots, the amount of people attending, or even the mechanical bull, I told them that I had lost a friend, a person who was really struggling, and that none of us saw it coming. I made it crystal clear that my goal was to make sure we could get any person struggling with depression all of the support that they needed. The meeting was a success, and the partnership with Horizon was there, but for some reason I was still feeling the pressure, despite all this progress.

The difference between this Fiesta Bowl and anything I had ever done up to this point, is that this time I felt the weight of the community, my family and my brothers. I felt the weight of making sure this event was a success, and that it honored Devin the right way. All of the promises made, that I could be "the guy" to step up and help others, and that I would do anything for them, all relied on me making sure I gave this thing everything I got. I had kept all of this inside since losing Devin, and did not want people to know I was feeling the pressure, or that I was struggling. I was supposed to be the kid people looked up to and I drilled the thought in my head that if they could not see me weak. These Saturday morning meetings became my only source of closure during the week. Other than that it was constant round-the-clock fear trying to make sure every detail was right. I had trouble sleeping and my eating habits changed, so even though my entire family was trying to help me delegate and make things easier, I still felt a greater weight on my shoulders to get this right.

"I'm Freezing My Ass Off Nick"

As the months went on, the excitement and hype continued to build, and progress was finally starting to show. By mid March we were locking up sponsors and businesses left and right to support us. The idea of pitching the dream to CEOs and perspective parents used to scare me, but was now a daily occurrence after school. We were getting big name sponsors and more people to believe in the mission. We were beginning to see that that little dream in the basement was starting to become a reality.

One of the things early on that my parents and I thought would be a good idea to help spread excitement for the Fiesta Bowl, was to have a photographer come in and take photos of all the players. Up to this point, the lid had been kept pretty tight on all the plans and progress we had been making. When I made a group chat with all the neighbors saying I needed them at my house for a photoshoot, they thought I was out of my mind.

It was a cold March day, and snow was hammering the dead end of Berryman Drive. My neighbor Jimmy had drove all the way from John Carroll University in Cleveland, to be here for this. We were going to each door getting all the neighbors. They all screamed, "it's 30 degrees out I'm freezing my ass off Nick." It was quite a sight, all six of us, garnered in our Fiesta Bowl uniforms, walking down the dead end in the bustling snow.

Everyone got inside and immediately started laughing. A media backdrop was in the middle of the room, just like all the professional sports teams used. However, what really surprised them was the six foot tall basketball trophy in the middle of the room. None of them really believed me when I had been claiming for months we were getting all of this, so it made the moment even more priceless to see the stunned look on all their faces. The photoshoot went off without a hitch. Everyone was having a good time and getting ready to leave, then I decided we needed to take one more picture.

The term, "The Fiesta Bowl is Family," was something that resonated with me, and something I truly believed in. I told all of the players that despite all the jokes, and all the crazy stuff that came with this event, we were really going to be able to help a lot of people. Each player received a warm up long sleeve, and on the back it read one single message: #DevinStrong.

We were doing our best at that time to be a stronger, more loving, and more open community. That meant, as individuals, doing whatever we could to be there for one another, a message that I tried to live by every day. So when we all turned our backs, each of us facing the camera with #DevinStrong showing, the message was clear: This was something a whole lot bigger than basketball, it was bigger than all of us.

"There's No Way That's Gonna Happen"

In life, no matter how much you are

tested, you can always count on the people

you love. Leaning on the people closest to me

had become something I was accustomed to

since losing Devin. I never was a kid to really

look to others for help, but I was starting to

open up to the idea as the Fiesta Bowl process

went on. I was going to need their support

more when it came to trying to convince

Canisius that the Fiesta Bowl was legit. Despite

all of the success we had been making, people

still did not believe any of this would happen,

from the administration to some of my classmates.

It was hard saying things like smoke bombs, mechanical bulls, and six foot trophies in a sentence and having people take me seriously. When I told fellow classmates about my ideas, I got laughed out of the room. They all said, "There's no way in hell you're having a mechanical bull and a food truck on your front lawn." When I mentioned my financial goal was to raise ten thousand dollars, even my closest friend Will came up to me and said, "There's no way that's gonna happen." It started to hurt me personally that there was so much doubt, even amongst my classmates, that this could all get done. I knew I had my core brothers

support for believing the mission, but if

convincing some Canisius kids was hard, the

administration would be a whole other animal.

When it came to convincing The System,

and everybody who doubted me, one simple

message was always in the back of my mind: I

could never let anyone tell me not to live my

dream. Convincing them that this dream could

become a reality did not happen overnight.

What started from the day I got back from

Christmas break, all the way through the

beginning of April, was three months of

convincing them all to give me a chance. Even

seeing Mr. Coppola in the hallway, I would

shout, "Something big is coming." I knew I was not going to be able to propose all of this to the administration without every single detail being covered, so before I left for Spring Break, I handed my proposal into the dean's office. Weeks went by without me hearing anything. It was as quiet as a church mice any time I brought up the Fiesta Bowl to them. I started to think to myself, "Was all of that work for nothing?" "Is the dream dead?" It all was starting to get to me that this emotional burden to honor my friend was never going to happen. Finally after almost three weeks of waiting for a miracle, Mr. Coppola told me to come to his office.

What I thought would be a fifteen minute conversation, turned into an almost two hour show down. It really was a testament to all the time put in planning and organizing, because for every question he had, I was able to respond with ease. Eventually as the meeting winded down, he asked me, "Nick, what would you like from us?" I told him I wanted to put on the best presentation anyone had ever seen, and that this was a chance to spread the word to our students that depression is a real problem. After some contemplating, Mr. Coppola and the administration said, "Alright Nick, I think we can get this done." The birds were chirping and the sun looked brighter. I walked out of that school and truly could not believe it. I was going to get the chance to tell the entire student body our story, and I went home that day knowing this would make or break everything I had worked towards for the past five months.

"You Only Get One Shot"

I was so excited that the school was giving me the opportunity to pitch the Fiesta Bowl, but at this point I knew it was going to be a lot bigger than just me. It was a very tense time at Canisius High School in the weeks leading up to the presentation. We all had been wearing sweatshirts with #DevinStrong written on the front for the past few months, and when the students came back from spring break, the school decided to take a different approach. With less than a month remaining in our senior year, the school said they would suspend any students wearing the sweatshirts.

I met with our principal, Mrs.Tyrpak Endres, and she explained to me that the decision was made after speaking to several psychiatrists and other schools that had dealt with situations similar to this. On a person to person level, I understood what she was trying to do and believed in the decision, but as a leader of the students I thought that with less than a month left, they should have let us finish the year off and not caused all this tension. The next day our principal went around classroom to classroom trying to explain to the seniors why the school decided to implement the sweatshirt-free policy.

Students walked out of the room while she spoke, there were shouting matches, and the seniors were never going to be able to be convinced that this was the right decision. I knew the Fiesta Bowl presentation was a week away, and that not only would I have the task of getting everyone on board with the Fiesta Bowl, but I had to try and heal a hurt and divided community.

The week leading up to the big presentation was a race to the finish line, making sure every single detail of the pitch would be perfect. It was my dad that told me, as I was preparing gift bags to be tossed out that, "You only get one shot Nick, make it count." That meant going classroom to classroom convincing every single teacher to be in the hype video, explaining to them that the school needed this. I promised Mr. Coppola that the gift cards would be tossed in a controlled manner, even though both him and I knew that it would be chaos. It meant explaining to Jayce that he would not get in any trouble for dunking over the dean in front of the entire student body. It meant even convincing my close friend Will McGennis to go to Lowes and get a piece of wood to break over his head. It meant getting Tom Blumberg to be the hype man and introduce me to the whole school. The hype for the event was starting to spread as teachers and students alike were all wondering what the hell "Revelas Student

Assembly" meant on the schedule. Even the CEO of Horizon Health Services was planning on being in the audience for the presentation.

What kept me up the entire night leading up to the presentation was that my family was going to be in attendance. The idea that my family, who had been sitting in meetings for this thing since December, who had heard the crazy stories about Hinchweek and SiutaFest at Canisius, and who put all their faith in the world this would get done from day one, were going to be in attendance. I had to make Horizon, my brothers, and my family proud, but most importantly, I needed to prove to the people that said I was nothing more than a "summer school reject" wrong. The entire

Fiesta Bowl was on the line, honoring my fallen

friend was on the line, and I knew I had an

opportunity to prove everyone who had

doubted me wrong in a few short hours.

"It's Showtime"

The morning started with my neighbor and I directing Mr. Batchen into the back parking lot of Canisius. You could see all the kids looking down from the homerooms as we were dragging the basketball hoop off the trailer, all shouting down, "It's showtime Revy!" I was not there for classes. I was not there for anyone else. I was there to try to do something no one had ever seen before.

After first period, they excused me along with a group kids to leave class and go set up the auditorium. Mr Coppola and Mr Flaherty walked in to the Auditorium to people setting up a media backdrop, installing the basketball hoops, a drum line practicing their verses, and kids running down the aisles in mascot costumes. It almost surprised me after seeing everything going on, that the first words out of their mouths were, "What can we help with Nick." My goal with the presentation was not only to get people on board with the mission, and show them a theatrical masterpiece, but to inspire change in our own school.

I went behind the curtains to put on my suit, and I could hear the drummers banging, the students roar when they came in the auditorium, and despite all of what was going on, I never doubted myself, or got nervous. I was talking about my lost friend, and speaking up about an issue, that although was very tough and personal, could really help others in need. When I heard my brother Tom Blumberg shout on the microphone, "Please welcome Nick Revelas," my head was clear, the gifts were in my hands, and I thought to myself, "Fuck the System," as I came running down that aisle.

All the work that had gone into making the presentation a success paid off. In January, my parents thought I was out of my mind when I bought the six foot trophy, but when I unveiled it in the Auditorium, the kids got up and roared. My classmates thought I was kidding when I said it would "rain gift cards," so people had no idea what to do when they were being tossed from every aisle in multiple directions. When I said the mascots would be playing basketball as the kids walked in, I got laughs in return, but it happened. Not a single person believed that star basketball player, Jayce Johnson, would dunk over Mr. Coppola, but nonetheless it happened. I have learned that visualizing success can be a tough thing sometimes. There will always be doubters, and there will always people trying to bring you down, but as long as I believed in myself, nothing could stop me from accomplishing my dreams.

Once it was finally all over it was like reality set back in. I was alone in the Auditorium, cleaning up the remnants of what had just taken place. Despite how well everything had gone, I still felt like there was work to be done. I did not go running up to see my parents, or go running out to see my brothers. I wanted to be alone, isolating myself from all the noise and excitement occurring in the halls. I knew everyone would come up to me and say "What a great job Nick," but it was as much my success, as all the students and teachers that helped make the video, the volunteers that had help set up all morning, and even Mr. Batchen driving the basketball hoop in. The idea of the Fiesta Bowl being a "family" once again sat in my head. All the people and the work that went on behind the scenes did not always get the credit, and I personally felt like I did not deserve any credit either until I accomplished what I had set out to do: honor Devin by bringing everyone together to make a real difference.

After cleaning the Auditorium, I went to a signing ceremony for my brothers, Will McGennis and Troy Gooch, in the gym. It was pretty funny watching the athletic director have to explain to the crowd in the room why Will had a cut on his forehead due to the wood. My head was pounding and I barely made it to the nurse's office explaining that I was not feeling well. I had given every ounce of energy

I had during that presentation, and it showed. Flushed, dehydrated, and tired, her and I both knew I had come to school to do what I set out to do, and she called my mom and allowed me to go home. I was laying on the couch resting, when my Mom finally saw me. She told me she was proud and said, "I really think you got em Nick, you're gonna get to 32 teams."

The most impactful part wasn't the dunk, the gift cards, or even the Fiesta Bowl. When meeting with Mrs. Tyrpak prior to the assembly, I told her that it was my intention to make a lasting impact on the school, and that this assembly was a whole lot bigger than basketball. Myself, Calogeno, Mrs. Tyrpak, and another senior, David Pfaff, decided on the idea of creating bracelets for all the students. One side said, "I'm here for you," and the other said "We fight together." There was a point in the assembly when I got to explain where we were going to donate the money to and who we were helping. It had been the craziest twenty minutes that the school had ever seen, but when I said, "We're going to tackle a bigger issue, and that's depression", you could hear a pin drop. It was the issue that all the kids knew was too real, especially without Devin in that Auditorium, and an issue that schools across Western New York wanted to shove under the rug. I got the chance to tell not only the kids, but the faculty and staff, that we all needed to work together to make

Canisius a more loving community. I ended my speech by saying, "We are one Canisius, we are one brotherhood, and the only way we will tackle depression is together."

Up to that point in my life, I had never been prouder of myself than when I saw the entire sea of people giving me a standing ovation. It felt like the entire school was on board with trying to create a real change. I went to bed that night and saw that over half the slots for the teams had already been filled. I knew I was one step closer to accomplishing the promise made in Calogeno's basement.

"Building The Dream Baby"

One of the most rewarding experiences, when it came to setting up for the Fiesta Bowl, was building the basketball hoops for the tournament. We bought all of the hoops from Dick's, and it seemed like a colossal task to have to build twelve of them. The Fiesta Bowl "family" grew a little bigger when myself, my close family friend Rob Logel, former swim teammate Zach Dellavilla, and one of my closest friends Tim Coudriet, were assembled to build the hoops. People from all different walks of life gathered together to accomplish one goal is what I thought the core of the

143

Fiesta Bowl was all about. Every Saturday morning for about two months, the four of us would gather in my front yard and build the hoops. There was no better way to start my Saturday than walking outside my house and greeting them all by shouting, "We're building the dream baby!"

Building the dream: three words that entailed everything that had led up to this point perfectly. Believing is seeing. First I had to believe that this would happen before I saw it, and all along the way I had to have faith in the process of getting there. It took less than three days for the tournament to get all thirty two of the slots filled. A couple months earlier the dream of a three on three tournament was just drawn up on a piece of paper. I was told by many to set the bar a little lower, at maybe sixteen or twenty teams, but I never had a doubt in my mind we would reach our goal.

The basketball hoops were just one small part of the setting up of the Fiesta Bowl, but it encapsulated the journey we had all been on the past few months. When we lost Devin, I lost faith in a lot of aspects of my life. I had lost faith in God, wondering why he had put my friends and I through all kinds of suffering the past few months. I had lost faith in others; it took a long time for me to try and trust other people. I also lost faith in myself, and my ability to help others. I always wanted to be "that guy" that people could come to if they needed anything, and at that point I thought I had done everything in my power to help others. When we lost Devin, I felt like I should have known something was going on, and put blame on myself for not seeing the signs leading up to it. I felt guilty and ashamed for not being there for one of my brothers who clearly was going through a lot.

Although all I had done was build basketball hoops for a tournament, it symbolized a whole lot more than that. It symbolized the entire community rebuilding itself after all the horrible events that had happened. We all wanted to come back stronger than ever. It symbolized trying to build a more loving and open world, a world that was dedicated to helping others suffering from depression. For me, building the hoops meant rebuilding all the faith I had lost over this emotional rollercoaster. The Fiesta Bowl was my channel to try and create change.

Building the hoops allowed me to reflect on my four years at Canisius. As I was garnered in the white tux, ready to graduate at the end of May, I looked back on everything that happened. I was a freshman who was scared shitless and did not know if he would even fit in at this big school. I was a sophomore and junior who -- despite being sent to summer school several times, received threats from my family to pull me out and send me to Amherst-- battled the adversity and continued on. I was a senior who at the start of the year did not really know his role amongst his friends, and was told, "College may not be an option for you."

I walked across the aisle. I was a graduate who would be attending college next fall, a feat which at times looked blurry and unlikely. I walked across the aisle, a leader amongst the students, and someone who cherished the relationships with his brothers more than anything. Canisius had taught me well in the classrooms, and at mass, but what I learned was how to be a better man. Every day I walked into that school and saw the sign, "Men and Women For and With Others." I didn't really understand what that meant early on, but after doing things like Hinchweek, SiutaFest, Latin De Mayo, the Walkathon, the Christmas Assembly, and the Fiesta Bowl presentation, I realized it's a whole lot more than words on a sign. Every time I wanted to try something a little different and shake things up, Canisius gave me the platform for every opportunity. I loved helping other people, and making them happy. Going to school every day meant a chance to put a smile on someone's face. I was grateful for the relationships I made, the memories that would last a lifetime, and the fact that they gave me a chance, after a ton of convincing, to pursue my dream with the Fiesta Bowl.

"It Takes A Village"

The week leading up to the Fiesta Bowl was a stress-filled, last minute push to try to get as much money as possible raised for Horzion Health Services and the Alzheimer's Association. A couple of nights before the big event, I decided to take a night off from all the stress and join my friends down in Ellicottville. It felt like an eternity since we had graduated. I had been so focused on the Fiesta Bowl stuff that I had not really seen any of them in weeks. I found it hard to even sit down and relax for a little bit, and people were starting to notice. Brothers like Jack Dallas and Will Lawley asked me if I was all good, and I would lie right to their face and say, "Yep, all good." I had not been good for the past few weeks, and all the pressure of making sure that the event was going to be a success led to me not sleeping and barely eating. However, I knew that this was what it took for me to make sure I gave everything I had to make the Fiesta Bowl work. I remember my very close friend, Delia, pulling me to the side saying, "Nick you gotta stop worrying about everything it's going to be great." Delia was one of the only people that believed in the Fiesta Bowl from day one. From the first day I showed her my plans to this point, she has always been supportive. When I pulled her to the side and told her that we were going to raise around twelve thousand dollars total, she was ecstatic. She and I both knew that ten thousand dollars seemed like a pipe dream back in December. The fact we had already passed the goal with checks still coming in was amazing. Everyone would have been satisfied with twelve thousand dollars, but I still felt like there was so much work to do. Even though the Fiesta Bowl was something that brought people together, I had set my goals so high that I felt I had to live up to my own standards and amaze everyone.

The day before the Fiesta Bowl was finally here, it really felt like all the pieces were falling into place. All the Saturday mornings full of plans and notes paid off. When I went to the church that day to set up, everything was running like a well-oiled machine. People were hanging up banners along the walls of church, setting up tents and chairs, getting the food truck and drinks in place, while others were lining the parking lot with duct tape. The idea of "family" was in full effect seeing, my mom, dad, sisters, and neighbors all doing their part to make sure this would all be done in time. It was while Jimmy and I were reviewing the tournament format with Pastor Steve, I got a call from Christina Pearl from Horizon. She said that Channel 4 was interested in doing a story on the Fiesta Bowl, not only having cameras at the morning tournament, but doing a one on one interview that night. Our little Fiesta Bowl, which three years prior was being played in front of a dozen people and some guys building my hot tub, was going to be on the news for all to see. I knew this would be a chance to tell people in our area all the adversity the community and I had overcome after losing Devin. I agreed to do the interview right away and my charisma grew, as more and more opportunities for awareness arose from the Fiesta Bowl.

The Fiesta Bowl's goal was to raise money and awareness for depression, and that message could have not come at a more relevant time. In the weeks leading up to the event, celebrities Anthony Bourdain and Kate Spade died by suicide, so getting the opportunity to go on the air and tell the whole community what we had overcome the last six months was extremely important to me. By the time I got back to my house, I knew that this was a whole lot bigger than a basketball game. My phone was blowing up with people who had seen the news. Neighbors were outside hanging banners and spotlights. There was a sponsored BMW on the front lawn, and tents lined the street. I thanked everyone for the help and told them all, "It takes a village to make this dream a reality." Jimmy and I walked in my backyard to my mom telling us that the GoFundMe was blowing up, and that we were going to reach an unprecedented number. I kept repeating to myself, "We're going to make an impact, we're going to make an impact." I went to bed that night, not nervous about what was at stake the next day, but excited to show everyone that had doubted me all of the extensive work that I had done.

"Bigger Than Us"

The morning of the big day was finally upon us, and Jimmy and I walked outside of our houses to a truly beautiful scene. The Dead End of Berryman was always the group of people that supported me the most. From spotlights being hung in the trees, to when I needed them the most after losing Devin, they were always there for me. To come outside and see car after car of people all heading to the church to volunteer was just another great example of the Fiesta Bowl bringing people together like a family. I remember turning to Jimmy and saying, "This is all a whole lot bigger than us." We pulled into the church and the cooks were setting up the food trucks, my sisters were loading up the coolers, and my mom was explaining things to everyone at the registration desk. All the courts were taped up, the volunteers were in position, and the kids were pouring in. Six months prior, the Fiesta Bowl was just some drawings on a piece of paper, and the idea of running a basketball tournament was deemed "impossible" by many, but the dream was finally becoming a reality.

The best part of the morning did not even include any basketball, and took place before a single ball was shot. Before all the festivities took place I got a chance to speak to all the players, a lot of whom were my close brothers. I went over all the rules and regulations, but with the news, my family, and Horizon watching, I got to tell them all that we were doing something a whole lot bigger than basketball; we were playing for Devin. After my emotion-filled speech, Christina Pearl from Horizon got up to speak to the kids. That day we were going to have fun, we were going to raise money, but the most important message was to try and remove the stigma that came with talking about depression. Seeing all those kids, and the long looks on their faces, I knew the journey we all had been on for the past six months. Seeing depression become an issue on the forefront of all these kids' minds, instead of being shoved under the rug, is what I always wanted. Since my days running Berryman Game Night, my goal was to always make people happy, to make a real difference. Tears streamed down my face as I saw it happen before my eyes.

Watching twelve games of basketball going on at once truly seemed like a work of art. Success can not be attained unless you put in the work, and the hundreds of man hours that went into making the tournament happen seemed to pay off at the end. We had overcome all the adversity and doubt that came with trying something that had never been done. We overcame acquiring insurance, finding a venue, buying the hoops, and creating the game format. All of this, a few months earlier, seemed completely out of my league, but the tournament went off without a hitch, and it was a massive success.

I got back home exhausted and barely able to move around. I only had a few short hours before Berryman Drive would be tested like never before with this night event. I laid down for a minute but could barely close my eyes. I was so nervous, saying to myself, "Would people even come?" "Was everything going to work?" "Would the game be close enough?" Despite all the success we had just had in the morning, I still doubted myself and everything we had done. It started to become a pattern that I really never allowed myself to just enjoy the moment and not worry about having to do the next thing. As I was laying in my bed, over twenty volunteers were outside, making sure that the final details were being put into place. I did not know what to do, so I closed my eyes, went down on my knees, and prayed that this would all work out.

"Oh It's A Show"

It felt like a scene out of a movie. I walked downstairs into the kitchen and saw all my neighbors in the make-shift locker room. Jimmy and Nick T were talking strategy, Owen was putting on his shooting shirt, and Tim was tying his sneakers. We all knew we were going to play terribly, but the fact that this many people would be watching, we knew we had to look the part.

When the event started four years prior, we were garnered in neon shirts, and played in front of no more than a dozen people. Making it so, when all of us players walked out of the tunnel and saw hundreds of people, we were taken back. It was a sea of people that shouted, "Give em hell Rev," every time I took a shot. The whole game was elevated to the next level because we had a professional DJ playing music to hype us all up. It was made clear from early on that this was not going to be a normal front yard basketball game.

After the warm ups we were sitting in the garage, waiting for my uncle John Murphy, the play by play announcer for the Buffalo Bills, to introduce Jimmy and I's teams. All you could hear roaring through the garage was, "Revy, Revy, Revy." I went up to Jim who was trying to motivate his teammates, patted him on the back and said, "Oh it's a show Jim." It was finally go time. Jimmy and his team were introduced first and I was sitting in the garage shaking with excitement. I thought about the journey I had taken to get to this point. The Fiesta Bowl was bringing light to a very dark place. Even though six months earlier, only a handful of people believed this could all happen, we were finally all here together.

It was time for my team to walk out. I looked out the garage door, saw the white smoke rising, and heard the crowd roaring. All the hard work was going to come down to this moment and I was ready to prove everyone wrong. When I came out, I came out running. I ran out of the tunnel to a breathtaking scene. The balloon arches towered over the driveway, the sponsorship banners encased the entire court. There was not a single patch of grass uncovered, as there was over 250 people on the lawn. In this moment I realized the system had finally been beaten. It was all finally happening. Without anything else to fix or work on, it was time to just play basketball.

The game, as expected, was full of missed shots, airballs, and people all wondering: "What the hell am I watching." I was extremely lucky that the game remained close throughout. It ended up coming down to the final seconds with Team Jimmy prevailing.

Even though the scoreboard read 32-31, I

knew I still had the opportunity to win the day.

Over the past few years, the Fiesta Bowl was

known for the open bar and the bad basketball.

However, besides all of this, at the end people

all gathered to hear me give a speech. Now I

don't know what caused this phenomenon, but

people knew they had to listen. I felt all the

pressure when over 250 of my closest friends

and family were waiting for me to come out of

my house and speak.

As I came out to speak, the laughter and

banter that had ensued the entire game, had

stopped. It was almost an eerie silence for

there being that many people. I knew that the first thing I had to do was thank the people that believed in this dream from the start. It's a tough pill to have to swallow, coming home from school everyday knowing so many people doubted that any of this could happen, but without my parents, and a few close friends always believing, something like the Fiesta Bowl could have never happened.

Next, I had to take care of the people that had supported me since the very beginning. The Dead End of Berryman Drive believed in me and my efforts, starting with Berryman Game Night in my hot, crowded, garage all those years ago. There was no greater moment then getting the opportunity to help one of our own, Mrs. Lasting. I brought up Dante, a kid who had always been there for me through the highs and lows, and announced that we raised almost five thousand dollars to help families like his all across Buffalo beat Alzheimer's together.

Then, it was time to fulfill the promise that was on the forefront of my mind since Calogeno's basement on that cold December night. We may have lost our innocence, and losing Devin may have knocked us down, but it's not about how we fell, it's about how we got back up. I knew me announcing some dollar amount would not bring back all we had lost, and it wasn't about the money. It was about raising awareness to create a better environment for those struggling with depression. When I brought the representatives from Horizon Health Services, I implored to everyone that the Fiesta Bowl is a stepping stone for how we could live every day in our lives. Despite all the adversity I had faced, all the people that doubted it could ever happen, and all the odds being against us, I was still able to fulfill my promise to beat the system when I announced the check was for fourteen thousand dollars.

With tears coming down my face after presenting the check, the crowd roared. I ended the speech with the four words that founded the very idea of the Fiesta Bowl: "Welcome to the Show." I dropped the mic, found my dad through the sea of people storming the court, and hugged him. The emotions just poured out of me as it felt like the burden of honoring Devin the right way was finally off my shoulders.

My head was spinning, I could barely recognize what was going on, and I found myself in the arms of Will Lawley and Charlie Desmond, the two kids that were the closest people I had, next to my family. They were screaming in my ear "You fucking did it Rev, you really did it." An entire community took a chance on me and believed in the dream that not many people thought could even happen. It didn't take me more than second to respond back, "No guys we did it."

"So What Now?"

Following the basketball game, there was a party in the backyard with my closest friends and I. Neighbors, brothers, and others, all gathered together having a great time celebrating what had just occurred. Where was I? I was sitting in my shed alone and away from all the noise. Despite all we had overcome and all the people we had proven wrong, I still could not simply enjoy the moment. I knew we had come so far. From an impossible dream to a imminent reality, it still felt like more had to be done. For the past six months it was a race to the finish. I was constantly trying to set the bar higher and help as many people as I could. To be told that I had done enough and that it was time to celebrate was something that I could never accept. I still felt like I had to help more people and make them happy. Well all these thoughts racing through my head at the speed of light, there was a massive celebration just fifteen feet away that I was not ready to face.

My close friends Delia, Leah, and Will had all come in to check on me, and as I sat in disbelief, a large roar was occurring outside. My neighbor Joe Miller, who was notorious for strolling around the Dead End of Berryman in a bikini, started screaming, "Nick's gonna be on the news turn on Channel 4." I appeared out of the shed and joined the mass of people heading inside my porch to watch. It was when I sat down and just took a minute to look around, when I realized that I was having deja vu. Seeing all my brothers and everyone I cared about huddled together, took me back the night we lost Devin in Calogeno's basement. There was a lot of pain in that basement, a lot of lost faces, and a lot of us questioning ourselves. Despite all the suffering we endured, we got through it together, because we were there for one another. So there we all were, six months later, gathered on my porch as one family, a group that had just overcome the biggest test that we would ever face. As everyone looked on toward the

TV, cheering and celebrating, I could not help

but think back to that dark day, and how much

light we had made out of it since.

In the months that followed, The Fiesta

Bowl continued to amaze many. Donations

continued to poor in as another thousand

dollars was raised for Horizon Health Services.

People called it "the hands down event of the

summer" and the gratitude from both charities

was immense. I had received hundreds of

calls, texts, and emails congratulating me on

what I had accomplished, but I still was asking

myself, "So what now?" I was always so in the

moment. I was so focused on getting myself

and everyone else to the destination. I had no idea where that was, but I knew we had to keep moving. The battle inside of me raged on for months about what more I could do. It still felt like we had so much more to accomplish, but with no clear way to get there. This thought destroyed my head, and it made me want to isolate and be by myself, rather than with others. That was until one text finally gave me the answer.

We were all heading back home from college for Christmas Break, and it was Calogeno who texted in our group chat that we would be gathering to honor Devin for the one year anniversary of his death. It was in that moment that I realized that this was the opportunity to finally gain closure, and give everyone a moment they'd remember forever. I Immediately reached out to him and said that I would love to be involved, and that I'd come up with something. The question was what would that be? I stayed up for nights on end trying to think of something that perfectly embodied everything we had all been through, something that would leave a powerful message for those who were closest to me. When I thought about my journey over the last year, and all we had been through, one message came to mind: finding light through all the darkness.

So there we all were, gathered in Calogeno's backyard, on another cold December night. This time, not brought together by tragedy, but united as one family that had overcome the toughest battle that "The System" had ever thrown at us. I passed out Chinese lanterns, which might I add are completely illegal in the state of New York, and told everyone that together we would light up a dark world. I looked around at the people that had really become my family over the last year, all smiling in awe as over forty lanterns lit up the dark winter sky. Most importantly, I was smiling along with them. As everyone was walking inside as the lanterns flew away, I finally let mine off. I sat there in the cold, alone, watching the light wane the further it went. Before I walked inside I got to say what had been stuck in my mind for months, "We did it Devin."

Losing Devin left us all in a dark, confused place, none of us sure what to really do. A wise person once said "Grief is the price we pay for loving, but we never stop loving". In the past year we never stopped loving, we were always there for one another, and we all came together and created something beautiful with the Fiesta Bowl. Not only did we bring light to our hurting community, but we brought light on the issue of suicide and mental health. In the end no matter how many people doubt you, say that you're not good enough, or say

it's impossible, you can always be the light in a

dark world.

"At the end of the day it's not about what you have or what you've accomplished. It's about who you've lifted up, who've you made better, and what you've given back"

RIP BONE.

Made in the USA
Middletown, DE
18 April 2019